John Cordner

The American Conflict

An address, spoken before the New England Society of Montreal, and a

public audience, in Nordheimer's Hall, Montreal, on Thursday evening,

22nd December, 1864. Vol. 1

John Cordner

The American Conflict
An address, spoken before the New England Society of Montreal, and a public
audience, in Nordheimer's Hall, Montreal, on Thursday evening, 22nd December,
1864. Vol. 1

ISBN/EAN: 9783337328375

Printed in Europe, USA, Canada, Australia, Japan

Cover: Foto ©ninafisch / pixelio.de

More available books at **www.hansebooks.com**

THE

AMERICAN CONFLICT:

AN ADDRESS,

SPOKEN BEFORE THE

New England Society of Montreal,

AND A PUBLIC AUDIENCE,

IN NORDHEIMER'S HALL, MONTREAL,

ON THURSDAY EVENING, 22ND DECEMBER, 1864.

BY REV. JOHN CORDNER.

Published by Request.

Montreal:
PRINTED BY JOHN LOVELL, ST. NICHOLAS STREET.
1865.

The following Address was spoken before the New England Society of Montreal, and a public audience, on Thursday evening, 22nd December inst., the anniversary of the Landing of the Pilgrim Fathers. The chair was taken on the occasion by the President of the New England Society. On the platform were seated the Presidents and official representatives of the various National Societies of the city—English, Scottish and Irish. The Address was spoken from detached notes; and having been requested for publication by the New England Society, and by others who heard it, the following report has been prepared from the notes, and from memory.

MONTREAL, Dec., 1864.

THE AMERICAN CONFLICT.

——o——

GENTLEMEN OF THE NEW ENGLAND SOCIETY :

As I came down here this evening through the deep snow-drifts, and an atmosphere some degrees below zero, the thought of the hardships of the Landing which this day commemorates, rose to greater distinctness in my mind. To the frozen shore of a northern wilderness, on a cold December day, two hundred and forty-four years ago, came that resolute band of English men and English women who laid the foundation of the Plymouth colony of New England. Inspired by a lofty idealism and firm faith in God, they were constrained, for conscience sake, to forego the comforts of their native and much loved home, and face the perils of the sea, and of foreign and unknown climes. Such men and women, such faith and fidelity to conscience, are eminently worthy of commemoration.

FELLOW CITIZENS OF MONTREAL :

When, on the day before yesterday, the Committee of the New England Society asked me to speak here on this evening, I at once acceded to their request. Up till a few days ago, they had hoped that Mr. George Thompson of England, who is now visiting America, would have been able to come to Montreal for this anniversary; but though much desiring to do so, Mr. Thompson found that his engagements elsewhere rendered his present coming impossible. Had he come I should have been his grateful hearer. The name of George Thompson has been long familiar to me, as that of one of England's most active public men, whose labors in parliament and out of parliament on behalf of the working classes, and the rights of labor, have commanded my attention and respect. I hold in my hand Mr. Thompson's letter to the President of the New England Society, express-ing regret that he is compelled to postpone his visit to Montreal. Thirty years ago, in a pre-vious visit to America, it was his privilege, so he writes, to speak at Plymouth on the anniversary of "Forefathers' Day," and it would have given him great pleasure to appear again here at a similar anniversary, after the lapse of a genera-tion. But as he could not come, I have consented to appear here at rather brief notice. I do not say this for any purpose of making the Society responsible for the imperfection of what I may have to say. I need not have consented unless I had chosen to do so. The choice of topic, too, was altogether my own. And for any merit or demerit in what I may say, I alone am answer-able. Under ordinary circumstances I should not have consented to speak. But the time is extra-

ordinary. In view of the existing excitement
caused by recent events, I felt that our fellow
citizens of the New England Society of Montreal,
ought to have their anniversary in some form or
other. The events just referred to have suggest-
ed the subject of my address. I propose to speak
on the American Conflict. Living as we now do
in the midst of an excitement resulting from the
civil war in the nation across our borders, and
some atrocities connected therewith having been
so recently brought to our own doors in a manner
to make us think of possible peril to our own
peace, it seems a fitting time to review, though
ever so imperfectly, the American Conflict in its
origin and purpose. Any review here made,
must needs be very brief. Nor is there anything
new to be said. Still, in view of the misappre-
hension incident to a period of strong excitement,
when various passions, prejudices and interests,
are called into play, it may be useful to recal some
facts connected with the origin of this disastrous
strife, and direct attention to the end proposed
by those who initiated the war. And here at
the outset I would say, that if my observation of
this matter had begun after the actual outbreak
of hostilities, and had been mainly directed to the
heroic qualities of the Southern people, their fer-
tility of resource in fighting against great odds,
their endurance against their more powerful anta-
gonist, their suffering on their own soil, through
the devastation of war; and all this while their cry

was, that they only desired to be "let alone" in the
assertion of their freedom and independence as a
separate nation, then it is likely that I should say
as so many have said and still say, "Let them
alone ; let them have their reasonable demand of
freedom and independence : why prolong a war so
sanguinary in itself, and so detrimental to a wide
range of interests at home and abroad ?" If, in
addition to this very limited observation of events
forced on me by the current chronicle of the daily
newspapers, I had any personal or class interest
in the palpable failure of a great fabric of popular
government, or if, consciously or unconsciously, I
yielded my judgment to the lead of those who
have such interest, then I should actively sympa-
thise with the South, which puts a ban on honest
labor, holding its laborers as chattel property, and
proposes to perpetuate a dominant oligarchy as
the ruling class.   But as my observation of events
goes far beyond the outbreak of this war, and as,
moreover, I have no interest at all in depreciating
the capacity of the people to take care of their
own affairs and govern themselves, as I can claim
no connection whatever with oligarchy or aristocracy, it being my great privilege to be identified
at every point with the industrial classes of society ; and as, moreover, I refuse to yield to any
leading, be it· ever so artfully tendered, which
has for its intention or its effect the depreciation
of honest and free labor—all this being the case,
I am compelled to other and different views and
conclusions on this matter.

THE MORAL ISSUE.

More than twenty-one years have now elapsed since I came from the mother country to this daughter land, and took up my abode in this city. And during all this period I have been an observer of the moral aspects of the political affairs of the United States. For it has been a marked peculiarity of the leading political questions of that country that these questions were inextricably interwoven with moral questions in which the whole civilized world took an interest. The marvellous expansion of commerce in the leading Southern staple, gave to slave labor a greatly increased value, and thus augmented to the Southern view the importance of negro slavery as a social and political institution; and this, while the tide of a more enlightened public opinion was rising against it every where else in America and Europe. The conscience of the Northern States was gradually aroused to the moral wrong of a system which reduced a man to a chattel, making men, women and children, things of bargain and sale, depriving them of the rights of marriage and the family, thus opening a way to moral degradation on all hands. Great Britain, after a lengthened agitation, and at a great cost of money, had wiped the stain of negro slavery from her West India colonies. And having done this, her people, comprising all classes, sent remonstrance after remonstrance across the Atlantic, urging the people

of the United States to deal faithfully with this national evil, nor halt in their agitation against it
until it should cease to exist. Thus stimulated from
abroad, as well as at home, the anti-slavery agitation acquired formidable proportions. The South
became more and more alarmed for the safety of
their " peculiar institution." While its importance
to them in an economic point of view increased year
by year, the feeling against it in the Free States of
the Union, and throughout the world, increased
year by year likewise. The preservation of this
institution, its extension and perpetuation, became
the central thought of the Southern mind. All
political questions were considered primarily in
their relation to this as the cardinal point. It
entered into all party combinations throughout
the United States, north and south, east and west.
This has been patent to every observer during the
past twenty years. As the grand moral issue involved became more distinctly revealed, rising
every year into clearer and more definite form,
it gradually disintegrated the existing combinations of party politics, based as they were on considerations of expediency or economics. A few
years ago it broke up the old and influential
Whig party in the United States. And more
recently, it has utterly demolished the old and
well-organised Democratic party. The thoughtful
observer, looking through outward events to the
moral forces which produce them, will see here a
steady upward tendency of the public mind to a

higher plane of civilization. All who have stud-
ied the moral struggle in England, led by Clarkson
and Wilberforce, and their cotemporaries, on behalf of simple justice towards a weak and oppress-
ed race, will be able to appreciate in some measure, but not to its full extent, all that is involved
in the gradually changed public opinion of the
United States. In England the influence of the
West India interest was powerful against Clarkson and Wilberforce, but it bears no proper com-
parison with the influences so various and powerful which the Southern interest could exert on
the general mind of America. In England the
movement on behalf of human freedom, was
jeered by an influential press, and its advocates,
including the most honored names in the land,
were mobbed in English towns. But the fidelity
of those honored men to their ideas of justice led
to a triumph for freedom throughout the whole
mind of the nation, which now stands as one of
the proudest traditions connected with the British
realm and the British name. A similar trial of
misconception, misrepresentation and mob violence, awaited the movement in the United States,
but on a larger and more determinate scale. In
America, there were political obstacles in the
way which did not exist in England. And these
obstacles not being rightly apprehended in England, it came to pass that English remonstrances
addressed to the people of the United States on
the subject of slavery frequently failed of their

purpose. But the honest desire to mitigate the
growing evil of slavery in the nation, made hope-
ful progress in the national mind of the American
Union. It came more and more to be regarded by
the people as a blot on the fame of their great
and prosperous country. It was felt to be a dis-
credit abroad, and a fertile source of dishonest
party intrigue at home. Then on moral grounds
it was seen to be without defence. The intense
anxiety of the Southern mind for its safety, now
so imperilled by having the attention of the
civilized world brought to bear more directly
upon it, culminated in fanaticism. The moral
discussion of the subject, so long dreaded and
evaded by the South, was now faced by them in the
spirit of a forlorn hope, and positions taken which
revealed the distraction of their moral conscious-
ness, and the distortion of their moral convictions.
" When the slavery question was first mooted in
" our national councils," says the Rev. Dr. Leacock
of New Orleans, in a sermon preached November,
1860, " we dreaded the consequences, and trem-
" bled at the bare mention of the subject; we stood
" aghast before our adversaries; and why? Because
" we were not so well informed on the subject of
" slavery as we are now ; many of us doubted whe-
" ther we could religiously hold our servant." This
moral doubt, he adds, made them cowardly, but in
the new light of the last few years, the doubt has
been dissipated, and now they feel that they can
hold their slaves; and this new moral certainty

which has come to them, has given them a courage
not felt before. The position now quite commonly
taken by the South is, that slavery is a divine
institution, existing there to-day by divine sanction, and for a divine purpose. It is affirmed that
the providential purpose of the South is to preserve,
extend and perpetuate it. Says the Rev. Dr.
Palmer, of New Orleans, in a sermon preached in
that city rather more than four years ago : " The
" providential trust committed to the South as a
" people, is to conserve and perpetuate the institu-
" tion of domestic slavery, as now existing." He
avers that in standing by this trust, they are defend-
ing the cause of religion. As the providentially
constituted guardians of slavery, he adds, " the
" South can demand nothing less than that it
" should be *left open to expansion, subject to no human*
" *limitations.*" This is the language of slave-holding
fanaticism, which could obtain no hold or hearing
outside of slaveholding limits, or slaveholding
influences. Fanaticism is a species of madness,
and, in this instance, it may be safely taken as
an illustration of the adage which makes madness
the presage of impending destruction.

THE POLITICAL ISSUE.

Here we see indication of that political issue
which now became inevitable. Aiming at the
territorial expansion of slavery, the South would
not only not allow any further limit to be placed

to its extension, but they would break down the
limitations already existing, and by law established, as a peaceful compromise of the matter so
long in dispute. More than forty years ago,
when Missouri—a part of the Louisiana tract
—was admitted as a State into the Union, there
was a lengthened and important debate on the
slavery question, which was brought to a close by
the adoption of a measure of compromise, known
as the "Missouri Compromise." Missouri was
admitted as a Slave State, but a line was drawn
north of Arkansas, northward of which it was
solemnly agreed that slavery should not be
extended. This agreement was enacted and rati-
fied in due form, and stood as the confessed law
of the land for more than thirty years. But the
restless and aggressive spirit of slavery became
dissatisfied with this established limitation, and
through various intrigues and party combinations
at the North, succeeded in breaking down the
Missouri Compromise. This was accomplished
during the presidency of Mr. Pierce, and thus the
way was opened for the unlimited extension of
negro slavery throughout all the territories of the
American Union. This act, which, however, was
only one of a series of aggressive acts on the part
of the Slave Power, aroused the people of the Free
States to a more united and determined resistance.
The effect of this was seen in the presidential
election of 1856, when Mr. Buchanan and Colonel
Fremont were the rival candidates. Mr. Buchanan

was the Democratic and Conservative candidate, so-called, prepared to conserve slavery, and, as a general principle, to be controlled by Southern influences. Colonel Fremont was the candidate of the party which aimed to exclude slavery from the territories. The popular watchword of this party was "free soil, free speech, free men, and Fremont." Its time for success, however, had not yet come. Fremont was defeated, and Buchanan was chosen President for the next four years. Meanwhile, the Free Soil party, now known as " Republicans," as distinguished from the " Democrats," were not idle. The disastrous influence of slavery in the National Councils became more fully developed as it saw the political dangers thickening around it. The imperious self-will, which comes from the habitual exercise of irresponsible power, the impatience of restraint which such power engenders, and the ready resort to violence which springs from familiarity with the plantation whip—all this was brought into the halls of Congress. A Massachusetts senator was stunned with a slaveholder's bludgeon in his seat in the Senate House at Washington. Southern communities publicly applauded the dastardly and ferocious deed. It became more clear to the mind of the Free States that there was only one course, viz : to check the encroachments of the Slave Power, and publicly pronounce Slavery a sectional, not a national institution. As another presidential election approached, the Republican party

organized for the contest, attempting no interfer-
ence with slavery where it already existed, thus
conceding the right of the several Slave States
to deal with it after their own manner, but
proposing to restrict it within its present limits,
and to prohibit it in future throughout territories
of the Union where it did not then exist. This
was the main issue presented at the presidential
election of 1860. Briefly stated, the issue was
this : the unlimited expansion of slavery, as
demanded by the South ; or its territorial limitation. This issue went before the whole United
States. Every State, North and South—from
Maine to Texas—went into the contest. All sent
their votes to Washington. And the result was,
that Mr. Lincoln, the candidate of the party for
the non-extension of slavery, was announced as the
constitutionally elected President of the United
States for the next four years.

THE ACTION OF THE SOUTH.

As soon as this announcement was made, the
South showed unmistakable symptoms of deep
dissatisfaction, and a determination to revolt.
Subsequent developments show us how these first
symptoms ripened into a formidable and wide-
spread insurrection, involving the nation in the
horrors of a civil war. Before Mr. Lincoln was
inaugurated, and while Mr. Buchanan was still
President, the national property at Charleston,

South Carolina, was seized, the national ships were fired upon in Charleston harbor, and other like acts of war waged upon the National Government. Then ordinances of secession were rapidly passed without consulting the people, a revolutionary Congress established, and an army of resistance raised. So that when Mr. Lincoln was inaugurated, and in advance of any overt act of his government in relation to the South, he found himself confronted by a formidable insurrectionary opposition. Now, had the South any just cause to initiate such civil war under the circumstances, and organize an army to carry it on as they have done to this day? I say, No. And in taking this ground, I waive all discussion of " State rights " so-called, as beyond my province and scope. My position is simply this : the South having gone into the presidential election of 1860, in common with the North, and all States of the Union, they were bound, in common with the North and other States, to abide peacefully by the constitutional result thereof. Whatever course they might take with respect to any future election, under any assumed right to secede, they were bound to this election, at any rate, by all constitutional and honorable obligations. And, having hastily and wilfully disregarded such obligations, *we are justified in holding them responsible for the origin of the present war*, and for the deplorable consequences which have followed it, and still follow it to their own nation, both North and South, and to other nations.*

I have just said that I here forego the discussion of State rights. Nevertheless, I may be allowed to remind you that all the seceding States do not occupy the same historical position. Of the States now insurgent, we find some, as Arkansas and Louisiana, whose soil and privileges were a purchased acquisition, made by the original States of the Union, the great bulk of whom are in and for the Union still. It was about sixty years ago that the United States purchased from the French, the large territory west of the Mississippi, known as the Louisiana tract, for which they paid between eleven and twelve millions of dollars, and assumed the payment of certain claims, making in all some fifteen millions of dollars, as the price paid. A portion of this purchased tract is now known as the State of Louisiana, which was admitted into the Union in 1812. Now what rightful ground can Louisiana

* A remarkable letter from General Lee has just found its way to the public through the columns of the London *Times*. It was written to his sister at the beginning of the Southern revolt: "My dear Sister," he writes, "the whole South is in a state of revolution, into which Virginia, "after a long struggle, has been drawn, and though I recognize no neces- "sity for this state of things, and would have forborne and pleaded to "the end for *redress of grievances, real or supposed*, yet in my own person "I had to meet the question whether I would take up arms against my "native State." Here is a confession from the leading general of the Southern armies, that he saw "no necessity" for the revolt into which he permitted himself to be drawn, and which has brought such disastrous consequences to the United States and to the world during the past four years.

have in saying to the bulk of the original States
who paid their millions of solid money for her soil,
and the advantages of outlet to the ocean
which it gives by the mouth of the Mississippi
river; what rightful ground, I ask, can Louisiana
have in saying to those other States : " I will
secede, and form an independent nation ; the
mouth of the Mississippi will be no longer at
the service of your nation except on my condi-
tions." Now, fellow-citizens, consider this matter
a moment : Here we are at Montreal, at the head
of the ship navigation of the St. Lawrence. Away
to the eastward of us, lies a large tract of Canadian
territory, rich in undeveloped resources. Away
to the westward, lie the great lakes, and the wide
stretching tillage lands of Western Canada. Now,
suppose the district of Quebec, including the outlet
of the St. Lawrence, were in the hands of a foreign
power, and that, in order to secure for ourselves
and our posterity an open transit to the ocean for
the various produce of our mines, forests and
tillage lands, we, the people of central and western
Canada, should purchase the district of Quebec at
of cost of some millions of dollars taken from our
joint treasury, what should we, the people of these
regions, say, if the people of the Quebec district
should, in a given number of years afterwards, an-
nounce that they had seceded, and that the mouth
of the St. Lawrence must henceforth be considered
by us as in the hands of a foreign power. I think we
should have a good many words with them before

we consented to any such transfer of purchased
privileges, as secession involved. And I think,
too, that if they took up the sword to fight out
this question of transfer by secession, we should
take up the sword, also, and keep it going until
we found out which of the two swords was the
longer and stronger.

Secession, according to the precedent the South
seeks to establish, means anarchy. It means
anarchy, not only in the United States, but
throughout this whole continent. If the Slave
States had a right to secede because they were
defeated at the polls in 1860, so likewise, had the
little State of New Jersey, and the two others
that were defeated in this year 1864. Now
Maine, Vermont, or New York, — any of the
States on our own border, may be defeated at the
next presidential election, four years hence.
Following precedent, they raise a tumult and
secede. Let the doctrine involved be practically
established, and how long would it be until we
should have it applied in Canada? If, instead of
national unity and political order on the other
side of the frontier, we had such political disinte-
gration and disorder, the contagion would spread
to our own side. It may be said that the political
pact in Canada is different from that existing
between the States of the American Union. But
how long would the letter of any political compact
be respected, if the public opinion became de-
moralized by familiarity with anarchy on the

other side of the frontier. I say, then, that secession, such as the Slave States have initiated, means anarchy. In logical sequence and natural consequence, it brings eventual anarchy to every political community on this continent, from the north pole to the tropic line.

THE ACTION OF THE NATIONAL GOVERNMENT.

When the purpose of the South became clearly revealed, the National Government was put to great disadvantage through lack of centralized power. The vacillating and feeble policy of President Buchanan, surrounded as he was in his cabinet by the active friends of the South, gave the Slave States time to gather and consolidate their strength. The cabinet influences at Washington favored them in various ways, among others by the almost wholesale transfer of the military stores of the nation, from Northern to Southern arsenals. When President Lincoln was inaugurated he found the departmental bureaus at Washington filled with public servants on whose fidelity to their public trusts he could not rely. Many were in secret, if not open sympathy, with those in revolt against his authority, and were not scrupulous in serving them, to the disadvantage of the National Government. The crisis was a new experience to the rulers at Washington. There was no adequate provision made for such a trial. Hence delay in action, when delay was highly detrimental and dange-

rous. The Southern people, more skilled in the
use of arms than the people of the North, could
place effective armies in the field more rapidly
than the North. Hence their early successes,
and the corresponding Northern defeats. The
National Government wished to avoid war. And
Mr. Lincoln did all that he honorably could do,
to remove the dissatisfaction and suspicion of the
South, and assure the Slave States of his just
respect for their rights under the Constitution.
He offered places in his cabinet to distinguished
Southern men—among others to Mr. Stephens, of
Georgia. In explanation of this it is to be borne
in mind that Mr. Stephens, though now Vice-
President of the Southern Confederacy, cast his
vote at first against the ordinance of secession in
Georgia. All efforts of Mr. Lincoln for concilia-
tion failed, because he did not concede the one
thing which the South required with respect to
slavery. Mr. Lincoln could not concede this
without betraying the confidence reposed in him
as Chief Magistrate by the Free North and West.
And all such efforts having failed, Mr. Lincoln
put forth his power to assert his authority, as
constitutionally elected Chief Magistrate, for pre-
serving the Union and the integrity of the nation
confided to his trust.

INCIDENTAL QUESTIONS.

Various incidental and complicated questions
arise out of this Conflict, tending to confuse foreign

judgment. For purposes of misleading foreign opinion they are readily available and have been freely used.

The Motive to War.

It has been said, for instance, that the maintenance of the Union was the motive to war on one side, and the desire for independence the motive on the other. Now, this is true, but it is far from the whole truth. There is enough truth in the statement, however, to satisfy any one who does not want to know anything more about the matter. Hence the confident clamor of superficial controversialists. There would be more truth in the statement if we should say that the North fought for the Union, although Slavery should be destroyed by the war, while the South fought for Slavery though the Union should be destroyed. Every discerning man, South and North, knows that this is the true state of the case. Mr. Spratt, of South Carolina, thus puts the matter in his letter of protest, written in February, 1861, against the decision of the Southern Congress with reference to the foreign slave trade. He regards the prohibition of this slave trade " as a great calamity," and a cowardly concession to the prevailing prejudices of the world. He avers that the slave breeding States " *have no* " *right to ask that their slaves, or any other products,* " *shall be protected to unnatural value in the markets*

" *of the West.*" " *The South,*" he says, " *is now in*
" *the formation of a Slave Republic* This, perhaps,
" is not admitted generally.   There are many
" contented to believe that the South as a geo-
" graphical section is in mere assertion of its
" independence......... . This, I fear, is an
" inadequate conception of the controversy.   ...
" .... *The contest is not between the North*
" *and South as geographical sections.* The real con-
" test is between *the two forms of society* which have
" become established, the one at the North and the
" other at the South." And he alludes as follows
to the prospects of an independent Slave Republic:
" Three years ago, in my report to the Commer-
" cial Convention at Montgomery, I said that Euro-
" pean States are hostile to the Union.   Perhaps
" ' they see in it a threatening rival in every
" ' branch of art, and they see that rival armed
" ' with one of the most potent productive institu-
" ' tions the world has ever seen; they would
" ' crush India and Algeria to make an equal
" ' supply of cotton with the North; and, failing
" ' in this, they would crush slavery to bring the
" ' North to a footing with them, but to slavery
" ' without the North they have no repugnance :
" ' on the contrary, if it were to stand out for
" ' itself, free from the control of any other
" ' power, and were to offer to European States,
" ' upon fair terms, a full supply of its commodi-
" ' ties, it would not only not be warred upon,
" ' but the South would be singularly favored—

" ' crowns would bend before her; kingdoms and
" ' empires would break a lance to win the smile
" ' of her approval; and, quitting her free estate,
" ' it would be in her option to become the bride
" ' of the world, rather than as now, the miser-
" ' able mistress of the North.' "

Mr. Stephens, of Georgia, Vice-President of the
Southern Confederacy, leaves the world in no
doubt about the origin of the war, and the
purpose of the South in waging it. "African
Slavery, as it exists among us," he says in his
celebrated speech after the adoption of the new
Southern Constitution, " was the immediate cause
" of the late rupture and present revolution.
" .... The prevailing ideas entertained by
" most of the leading statesmen at the time of
" the formation of the old Constitution were, that
" the enslavement of the African was in violation
" of the laws of nature; that it was wrong in
" principle, socially, morally, and politically. It
" was an evil they knew not well how to deal
" with, but the general opinion of the men of
" that day was that, somehow or other, in the
" order of Providence, the institution would be
" evanescent, and pass away. This idea, though
" not incorporated in the Constitution, was the
" prevailing idea at the time. The Constitution,
" it is true, secured every essential guarantee to
" their institution while it should last; and hence
" no argument can be justly used against the con-
" stitutional guarantees thus secured, because of

" the common sentiment of the day. Those ideas,
" however, were fundamentally wrong. . . . .
" Our new government is founded upon exactly
" the opposite ideas. *Its foundations are laid, its*
" *corner-stone rests, upon the great truth that Slavery,*
" *subordination to the superior race, is the natural*
" *and moral condition of the negro. This our new*
" *government is the first in the history of the world*
" *based upon this great physical, philosophical, and*
" *moral truth.*" Yes, Mr. Stephens, it is the first,
indeed, and I think it will be the last!

So thoroughly was it understood throughout
the South by the leaders in the war movement,
that the preservation and extension of slavery
was the purpose of the war, that we find sus-
picions cast upon the fidelity of those parts of
the South which had not a vital interest in
slavery. Thus a writer in the Augusta (Ga.)
Chronicle says, " Disguise it as we may, the great-
" est danger to our new Confederacy arises, not
" from without, not from the North, but from our
" own people. . . . The indications are, that
" organised, if not avowed opposition, to the new
" order of things, may arise in States or parts of
" Southern States *not vitally interested in the slavery*
" *question.*"

Suspension of Constitutional Rights.

It has been said, too, that Mr. Lincoln's rule
was despotic—that constitutional liberty was
restricted by suspension of *habeas corpus* in some

cases, and strict dealing with the press. But a state of civil war puts constitutional rights in abeyance if this be found necessary to the public safety. Can any one doubt that, if the British Government found itself seriously confronted with armed, insurrectionary opposition anywhere within the limits of the United Kingdom, it would hesitate to suspend constitutional rights and interfere with personal liberty to any extent demanded by considerations of public safety and by the exigency of the occasion. Of course such suspension should only be had in the last resort, but of the last resort the government itself must be the judge. I shall not refer here to the notions of liberty held at the South. In the Slave States during their most peaceful times, there never was freedom of speech or of the press.

The War Tedious.

It has been further said that the war is an atrocious one in its methods, and that, moreover, it is tedious in its operations, and long in coming to a conclusion. Now, I say that all war is atrocious. The deliberate killing of men is atrocious work. John Wesley made a famous aphorism concerning slavery, affirming it the " sum of all villainies,"—and it was Robert Hall, I think, who made the aphorism concerning war, that it was " hell let loose." Yes, all war is atrocious. And the nearer we are to it in time and space, the more atrocious it appears. Then, as to the war

being tedious, certainly it is so, but all wars, where
the opposing forces bear any due proportion to
each other, are likely to be tedious. *It is much
easier to begin a war than to close one.* If the
South had duly considered this before firing her
first round shot, it would have spared the world a
great deal of anxiety and sorrow. Look at the
history of the more recent wars of the world.
Take the war for the occupation of the Crimea, a
territory about the size of one of the smaller States
of the Union. It took four nations of Europe
combined, including Great Britain and France—
it required the combined power of these four
European nations steadily exercised for about two
years before they dislodged the Russians. Take
the European peninsular war in the earlier part
of this century. Was it not in 1808 that the
French took Madrid, and was it not 1814 before
even the genius of Wellington, supported by the
allied armies, was able to drive them out of
Spain? Thus it took the allies under Wellington some six years to expel the French from a
Kingdom not much larger than the single State
of Virginia. War, indeed, is a tedious business,
and specially does it appear so when it presses
immediately on any of our own interests.

Is Popular Government a Failure?

Then, again, it is said by some that this civil
war decides the question as to the permanency of
the popular form of government adopted in the

United States—a government of the people by the people—administered according to republican forms. "The bubble has burst," exclaims an honest tory gentleman in one of the houses of the British Parliament. And so say a great many others, who had better hopes of the result of the great governmental experiment in the American Union. Now if we judge too hastily in this matter we may judge foolishly. If we cannot exactly look at the exciting events of our own day in the dry light of past history, let us at least pause and collate the past. Look at the history of the United Kingdom of Britain and Ireland. View it in connection with the English Monarchy, going back to the Norman Conquest. This brings us to the eleventh century. From that time to the present counts eight centuries. Now within these eight centuries of British history we may find an average of five intestine wars to each century. And if reckon from the end of the fourteenth century to the end of the eighteenth, we shall find each century showing an average of seven. Some of these were closed in a year, others not for ten years. Yet the British monarchy has not proved a failure, notwithstanding all these intestine troubles, but has shown itself a great and visible success. As compared with the maturity of Britain, the American Union is still in nonage. It is not a hundred years old. A century in the life of a nation is as a decade in the life of an individual. A giant youth in lusty life is

prone to say and do many things which the
staid decorum of mature age will be likely to con-
demn. But we must not judge finally of the
character of the man until the farther develop-
ment of the youth. I say, therefore, let us wait
until the completion of the first century of the
American Union before we pronounce definitely
upon its failure.

Popular Government in Divers Forms.

Let us not talk rashly in this matter lest we
should be found talking against ourselves, and
bearing witness against our own best hopes and
interests. Our fathers in the " old country " suf-
fered much, and struggled long against established
aristocratic pretension, to obtain for us, their
descendants, our just share of influence in the
national councils. Popular government, I define
as a government of the people, by the people.
Now this is what we have in Canada. With us,
however, it is administered under the form of
limited monarchy. But the difference here, as
compared with the government of the United
States, is formal, rather than substantial. Between
a limited or constitutional monarchy, and an unlimited or absolute monarchy, the difference is not
only formal, but essential. In the case of absolute
monarchy, the rule is arbitrary, as by the will of
the sovereign. In the case of limited monarchy,
the rule is constitutional, as prescribed by the
law of the land. As between an absolute and a

limited monarchy, therefore, the difference is seen to be essential. But as between popular government administered under republican, and under limited monarchical form, the difference is mainly formal. In both cases the people at large hold a controlling power in the government,—a power, I mean, sufficient to control the Executive, whether crowned or uncrowned. In Great Britain the representatives of the people hold the purse of the nation, and the crowned Sovereign has to ask them for the money needed to defray the expenses of the State; and this they may give or withhold as they deem best. To withhold the supplies, which they have the constitutional power to do, is to render the monarch powerless. Within the limits of the British Isles, as represented at Westminster, the territorial nobles exert a commanding, but still a restricted influence in the government. The history of the present century, however, shows the steadily increasing influence of the popular element in the government, and a corresponding decrease in the influence of the territorial aristocracy. This change is going on peacefully, and in virtue of a law of social progress, which, under the well-balanced institutions of Britain, has scope for that gradual expansion and adjustment to actual social necessities, which give stability to every step. But in these British American Provinces, where this class of territorial nobles does not exist and cannot exist, the influence of the people is more immediate and direct on our govern-

mental working. With this modification of our
institutions, resulting from the fixed necessity of
our position, our government becomes substantially
similar to the government of the United States,
though formally different therefrom. If, therefore, we rashly join in depreciation of popular
government, or follow the interested lead of those
who cry against the fitness of the people to govern
themselves, we may come to find that we have
been speaking against ourselves, and against the
best interests and privileges of our posterity. In
all popular forms of government, indeed, whether
administered under monarchy or republic, there
will be found much to deplore through the igno-
rance of multitudes who exercise an influence at
the polls. But this evil the more intelligent
classes must strive to diminish by elevating the
intelligence of the masses. This involves a faith-
ful and persistent attention to the cause of popular
education, without which no form of popular
government can exist with advantage or safety.

British Monarchy Stable, because Popular.

I have said that the British monarchy is no failure, but a success, notwithstanding its many intestine wars. But it would have been a failure
if it had resisted the just claims of the great body
of the people—your fathers and mine—to their
fair measure of influence in the national councils.
It would have been a failure if its settled purpose
had been to restrict human freedom, instead of
enlarging it. The strength, stability and perma-

nent success of the British monarchy are mainly due to the popular element by which it is sustained, and to the confidence with which it is regarded by the great body of the people. And with respect to the civil wars which have distracted the British realm, some of them were much longer in duration than the American civil war up to this time, and quite as fierce. That which was inaugurated in Ireland by More and O'Neil in 1641, lasted ten years. Meanwhile England and Scotland had their civil wars also. The active strifes of the English Roundheads and Cavaliers of that period were of a more sanguinary sort than those of the present Republicans and Democrats of the Free States of the American Union. And as compared with the pitched battles and bloody fields of those English contesting parties, the peaceful contest at the ballot-box last month between the two political parties throughout the Free States of the American Union, stands in sublime and instructive contrast. That contest on the eighth of November last, when millions of freemen, under pressure of a most exciting issue, cast their votes at the polls as peacefully as quiet villagers on a holiday, presents a spectacle for the world to admire, and bears more emphatic witness for the stability of popular government than all the victories of Grant and Sherman.

Historical Precedents.

It is to be borne in mind that, notwithstanding

the internal strifes in England, the insurrection in
Ireland was not lost sight of, but quelled by the
strong arm.   Then came confiscation of estates, to
the great grief of old Irish families.   Now if the
Free States, through the national government of
the American Union, should persist for ten years
toward the suppression of the insurrection of the
Slave States, and should in the end confiscate the
plantations, it will be seen that they have historical precedents bequeathed to them from the joint
English ancestry of North and South.   And I am
sure that under a changed system of labor, where
the tiller of the soil should work under the stim-
ulus of the paymaster's purse instead of the over-
seer's lash, the laborer would have nothing to
deplore.

President Lincoln.

Let us hope, however, that the war will not be
of much longer continuance.   The re-election of
Mr. Lincoln, by revealing the settled purpose of
the Free States to put forth their combined power,
may hasten its close.   Mr. Lincoln has had the honor to receive a large measure of abuse from the
enemies of popular government and the foes of free
labor.   And others, not exactly of this class, have
joined in the storm against him, being swept into
it by the current.   For myself, I am glad of his
re-election.   I regard him as an able and honest
magistrate, doing his duty faithfully under circumstances of various difficulty, such as few of us

who live more at ease can adequately understand. Mr. Lincoln began life as a man of hard-handed toil, and he is still a toiling man, though his hard work is now of the head. There are territorial nobles in England, and large planters of the South, whose early leisure for study, and more careful training in statesmanship, might have qualified them more eminently for such a chair as that which Mr. Lincoln occupies. But for one man of these classes who would have discharged his great trusts better, and brought more sagacity and integrity to the high task, I think it likely there would have been two, or perhaps ten, who would have performed the presidential duties a great deal worse. What if he did, in early life, earn his living by handicraft. Shall I respect him the less for this? Nay, but more. The main question for me is: was he honest in his handicraft work? And I am sure he was. I have never seen Mr. Lincoln; but what if his hands are hardened with honest toil. Should I approach him as President of the United States with less respect on this account? Certainly not. I should approach him with as much respect as if he had the blood of the Courtneys and Montmorencys and Howards, all flowing in his veins. And I should certainly approach him with much more respect than if he were the owner of the largest plantation in Virginia or Louisiana, where a thousand unpaid slaves toiled perforce for his benefit, and whom, by his word or sign manual, he could send to the auction

block to-morrow.   All honor, then, to honest
Abraham Lincoln, President of the United States,
and President-elect of the *Free* United States of
America.   [Here the speaker was interrupted by
prolonged applause.]   I hope the war will be
brought to a close long before the end of his second
term.   Would that it could be closed before the end
of the first six months thereof.   Would that South
and North should put foot to foot on the neck of
Slavery, the cause of their strife, and rejoin hand
and hand together in a common interest and a common hope, and that peace might be thus restored.
No one desires peace more strongly than myself.
But if this cannot be done, I see no immediate way
to the much desired peace, except the party who
first took up the sword shall be the first to lay it
down.

DUTY OF CANADA.

And now I approach a matter which directly
touches our own territory, interest and honor.   It
is to be kept in mind, fellow citizens, that the de-
clared policy of the Queen's Imperial Government
in reference to the disastrous civil war in America,
is neutrality and non-intervention.   It remains
for Canadians, as good subjects, not to compromise
this policy, or embroil Great Britain for the benefit of the slave institutions of the South.   According to present appearances, a continued policy of
non-intervention on the part of foreign powers
will ensure the speedy and irretrievable downfall
of slavery on this continent

The Raid on St. Albans.

You know how much our community has
been excited, and is still excited, by the ma-
rauding and manslaying at a peaceful village
on our borders, and the unexpected and un-
fortunate result of the judicial investigation
relating to the arrested parties. That result is
felt to be very humiliating to us as a people.
When the intelligence of the robbery first reached
this city, there was only one opinion as to its
atrocious character. This was subsequently modi-
fied with a portion of the community through the
plea set up in defence of the prisoners. The
simple facts of the case may be thus stated. A
band of twenty or thirty men entered the village
of St. Albans, Vermont—a quiet, unarmed, unsus-
pecting village—five or six hundred miles from
the nearest seat of actual war. These men came
into the village separately, and in the character
of ordinary travellers, taking lodging in several
hotels, and registering false names there. At a
certain hour on a given day, they went in com-
panies of three or four each, into the village
banks, as for an ordinary commercial purpose.
They enquired the price of gold, as if they had
some money-changing business to transact. Then,
watching their opportunity, they raised pistols,
after the Turpin fashion, to the head of the clerk
or cashier, and rifled the bank vaults. Meanwhile, other persons of the same band were putting
pistols to the heads of hostler boys in the livery

stables, and stealing the horses. Swinging themselves and their booty rapidly on these stolen
horses, the whole band started away at a gallop,
firing pistols on every side. One man passing
quietly along the village street was killed by the
shooting, others wounded, and a little girl by the
rural wayside struck by their bullets. In this
fashion they gallopped a few miles, across the border of our neutral territory, where a portion of
the gang was arrested, and made disgorge their
booty. And thus arrested, when brought before
the magistrate, they have the face to plead,
through counsel, that in the eye of the law they
are to be regarded as a—retreating army! For
such in substance is their plea. A retreating army,
indeed! Why if the worst enemies of the South
wished to caricature their warfare, they could not
do so more effectually than by this plea.

Lawful and Unlawful Use of Statute Law

I will make no imputation against the two
functionaries through whose precipitancy of action
these marauders have been allowed, on a technical
point, to escape with their booty. But this I will
say, that statute law is of no avail for good to any
community, if such law be not used lawfully.
For there is a lawful and an unlawful use of law.
I should not think of citing the Apostle Paul as
legal authority, but I have no hesitation in refer-
ring to him as moral authority. He writes that
" the law is good, if used lawfully," thus indicat-

ing that there is a lawful and unlawful use of law. All statute law is a standing token of the imperfection of human society. If human society were perfect, we should have no need of statute law. But statute law is useless, and may be worse than useless—it may be made instrumental in preventing, rather than in promoting justice—if the interpretation thereof be not controlled and directed by thorough respect for moral law. The interpretation and administration of statute law, lacking this, degenerate into mere intellectual dexterity, which, again, through pressure of low motives, may descend into a base game of trick. In all matters of statute law, municipal or national, and of international treaty stipulations, it is safe to say generally, that " that which is best administered is best." An honest purpose in the interpreter and administrator, is an absolutely requisite guide to a just decision, and an honorable administration of the law.

Transfer of the Seat of War.

In the western prairies, when the fire lights up the tall grass, and the wind sweeps it along in swift and terrible destruction, the settler finds his safety in lighting up another fire in another part to be carried along by the same wind. In the field of international politics, the process may not be precisely the same, but results may be produced substantially alike. There is a great war raging in the South, and it would undoubtedly suit the

interest of some, if the fires of war could be lighted
up here in the North, so that the destroying
armies operating there should be drawn elsewhere.
If, through any well-concerted intrigue into which
any portion of our community, be it ever so small,
or uninfluential, could be drawn consciously or
unconsciously to participate—if, through any such
intrigue, a combination of circumstances should be
produced which would light the fires of war in
the North, it is easy to see how well this would
suit the present exigencies of the South. If
General Sheridan, who, I am told, is a fellow-
countryman of mine, could be transferred with
his army from the Shenandoah valley to the
valley of the St. Lawrence, it would be a sensible
relief to the people of Virginia. But though I
should gladly welcome able Irishmen coming into
Canada, I wish to see them come with peaceful
intent. The Irish can dig well, as well as fight
well, and I desire to see them come to dig our
mines, fell our forests and till our soil. Here
they can have farms of a hundred acres or a thousand acres, with no landlord to grind or harass
them. Here every capable and industrious man
may be his own landlord. There is plenty of
room for all such who come, and a great deal to
spare besides. Or, if General Sherman, who has
just marched a flying column of forty or fifty
thousand men some three hundred miles through
the heart of Georgia, should, as the result of any
intrigue or combination of circumstances, have

his face turned northward, and his flying column carried three or four hundred miles into the heart ·of Canada, it would be a great relief to Georgia just now, and to the two Carolinas. If this, or any such movement, could be ensured, then other moves might be expected to follow. The British West India squadron, or some other British squadron, would move on New York or Boston. Then Farragut, Dahlgren, or Porter, would move on the British squadron. This would uncover the Southern seaboard, and open the ports of Charleston, Savannah, and Wilmington. Then might Mr. Davis and the men at Richmond rejoice. They had transferred their game of war into other hands, to be played out upon another board. Now they would be more likely to be "let alone" in the accomplishment of their purposes. Now they might look after their lost slaves, and gather up the million fetters broken during the war in the South. Now every round shot booming from a British gun against the Free States, would be as the stroke of a heavy hammer rivetting anew the manacles on the African, throughout all the wide territory, from Mason and Dixon's line to the Mexican borders. And who should have to pay and to suffer by such transfer of the war from South to North? You and I, fellow-citizens, all the people of Canada, and our relatives and friends, besides,—our fellow-subjects in the mother country. The bank robbery at St. Albans, and the Southern plots on our upper lakes, have al-

ready, it is said, involved Canada in an ex-
pense of nearly half a million of dollars. This
you and I and all Canadians will have to pay.
But this will not compare as a drop to the
bucket, to what we shall have to pay if an international war should be inaugurated through
Southern intrigue. In such case, what would
Canadian banks be worth? or Canadian shipping,
or property of any kind? Our relatives on the
other side of the Atlantic are already taxed enough,
without having to pay any more to equip naval
armaments to operate against the Free United
States for behoof of the Slave Confederacy. And
whatever certain classes of society there may desire—those I mean who desire to see a case made
out against the cause of popular government, or
who, possessing millions of money, have, through
the misleading reports of " Times' " correspon-
dents, invested some of their millions in Confederate stocks—whatever such classes may desire, I
am sure the great masses of the people in the
British islands desire no such war for any such
purpose. " Behold how great a matter a little
fire kindleth." Jail junketting in Montreal with
bank plunderers, and Southern sympathies stimulated by more elegant private hospitalities—these
social processes may be freely used for political
ends, and one may see the fruit thereof in the
expression of public opinion. A portion of our
press may do the work of the Slave States by
blowing hot and cold at a moment when a blast

of unqualified indignation alone should be given, or by a continued course of irritating insult towards the Free States. Edge tools in the hands of wise and skilful men are useful. But edge tools in the hands of fools or children, or those who do not know, or do not care what mischief they work, are not useful, but very dangerous. In such hands, the glittering playthings may be made to inflict wounds deep and disastrous, and very hard to be healed.

Southern Agents in Canada.

We are told, through a portion of our press in the interest and confidence of the Slave Republic, that influential Southern gentlemen residing among us give their assurance that our territory shall not be insulted, nor our peace put in peril. This assurance is gracious, and ought to be gratifying. But for my part, I do not want to hear any such assurances. Southern gentlemen who are here, are here on a neutral territory, whose laws they are bound to respect, and must be made to respect, if they will not be bound by the obligations of honor. The flag which symbolizes the British nationality is never without sufficient authority to effect this. We offer asylum in Canada to poor and rich alike, to the slave and the master, recognizing the freedom of one as well as the other, within the limits of our law. And if agents of the Slave Confederacy frequent our cities and traverse our highways of travel in pursuance of their mission, and promoting plots to " make European civiliza-tion shudder,"* they must, and I think will be looked after. The Canadian people have no desire that the British Empire should be drawn into a war which must be fought on their northern soil for the benefit and relief of the slaveholding interests of the South. If this dreadful strife must go on, let it be kept outside of our borders. Such, I hold to be the view of the Canadian people, and their Provincial Government. I have confidence in the fixed purpose and good faith of our Canadian Government in this grave matter.†

The Free States our Neighbors and Natural Friends.

We have no desire to quarrel with the Free

---

* Mr. Sala, in a letter to the London *Telegraph*, speaks of a Confederate agent whom he met on the Railroad, a few miles from Montreal. He told me, writes Mr. S., " that the St. Albans raid was only the first of a series of similar enterprises which were already cut and dried, and which were to be brought to maturity in the event of Mr. Lincoln's re-election, during the winter months. He said that he could com-municate by means of an impenetrable cipher with every city in the North, and that he had means at his command for causing the outbreak of incendiary fires in New York, Boston, Philadelphia, and Baltimore, and for forcing gold up to four hundred before the 1st of January next. 'In fact, Sir,' he concluded, ' we shall do such deeds within the next three months, as shall make European civilization shud-der.' Thus far the Confederate agent. I violate no seal of confidence in repeating this conversation, which took place in a railway car, on the way to St. Johns, Canada, where the preliminary examination of the raiders was to take place before the British authorities."

† Several of the liberated raiders have been re-arrested, including the leader, who was taken by the Government police about three hundred miles from Montreal, on the way to New Brunswick. While these sheets are going through the press, an investigation of this case is going on before one of the judges of the Superior Court, which, doubtless, will lead to a decision on the merits.

States of the North. They are our neighbors and
natural friends, bound to us, as we are to them, by
the reciprocal ties of amicable commercial inter-
course. With them, as with us, free labor is
respected, and the honest tiller of the soil has the
status of a man and a citizen. With them, and
with us, the word liberty has the same meaning,
involving the right of poor and rich, black and
white alike, to the disposal of their own persons,
of their personal ability and exertion, and of the
fruits thereof. In the vocabulary of the Slave
States, when they cry for liberty and independence, we know that they mean only license to
hold the poor in bondage, and rob the tiller
of their soil of his first rights as a man. The
traditions and policy of our mother country have
been steadily on the side of personal liberty.
And this, which is one of her most glorious
distinctions, has been a cause of constant hos-
tility towards her by statesmen and people of
the Slave States. Was it not the senator from
Mississippi who cracked his grim jokes at the
" crocodile tears " of English investers who
honestly bought, and paid for those Mississippi
bonds which were dishonestly repudiated—was
it not Mr. Jefferson Davis who did this thing,
the man who is, and has been from its beginning,
the President of the Southern Confederacy?
There was another Southern senator, who, to
irritate Old England, said her ships should be
swept from the seas; and to irritate New England,

said he should call the roll of his slaves on Bunker Hill,—and the man who said these things, was made the first Secretary of State in the Southern Confederacy. And when the heir to the British Crown visited the United States, a few years since, and received ovations of welcome in the leading cities, worthy alike of guest and host, it was reserved for one city in the Union to insult him, to hustle his suite in the public streets, and put contempt upon his Royal Mother's name,—and that city was Richmond, Virginia, now the capital of the Southern Confederacy. The Free States, and not the Slave Confederacy, are the natural allies of our mother country, the Free United Kingdom, where free labor is established and encouraged, and where the forced and unpaid toil of slaves is abominated.

Our Means of Defence.

Allow me to refer to one thing more before I sit down. Our people have been talking a good deal of late about our means of defence, as against our neighbors, on the other side of our long frontier. Fellow-citizens, our best defence is very close at hand. The Chinese method is a poor shift at best. It is said they blow horns, drum up all sorts of discordant noises, and yell defiance at their approaching enemies, in order to inspire them with terror. This is not a very rational or dignified method, and we soon discover that it is only a puerile way of trying to conceal weakness, and

hide their *fear of being considered afraid.* It is
the poor device of a poor form of cowardice.
We, Canadians, do not use Chinese blowing horns,
but if our mind is of the oriental type, we may set
up our clatter, and howl our defiance through the
trumpets of our daily newspapers. Our true
defence, as I have just said, is very close at hand.
I hope we all read the Bible. It is a wonderful
storehouse of wisdom for all emergencies. There is
a saying there by the Hebrew sage and preacher,
and it is this:—" Wisdom is better than weapons of
war." We read there of a little city against
which a mighty force came up to besiege it, and a
poor man delivered the city by his wisdom.
Therefore, saith the Bible sage, " Wisdom is
better than strength ;" " Wisdom is better than
weapons of war." And this wisdom may be shown
in the manifestation of a peaceful spirit, and of an
honorable purpose to fulfil, in all good faith, our
treaty stipulations with our neighbors. It may be
shown by our observance as dutiful subjects, of our
Queen's proclamation of neutrality, and by refus-
ing to sanction, directly or indirectly, any overt
act or implied purpose which would embarrass our
Queen's Government, or embroil in war the great,
industrious, peaceful and prosperous empire, with
which it is our privilege to be connected. It may
be shown by our fidelity to the noblest traditions
of that empire which forbids us to aid or abet, by
word or deed, the iniquity of slavery, or prop its
falling fortunes on this continent. It may be shown

by our love of human freedom, in our cherishing
the spirit thereof, and in our living desire that
all men should be free. It may be shown through
our respect for honest and honorable toil, and our
pronounced desire that the honest toilers in all
lands, whether they be black or white, shall receive an honest wage for their toil, and enjoy as
their indefeasible right, all the privileges of
Christian men. " Wisdom is better than weapons
of war;" and such wisdom as this, I hold to be the
bounden duty of Canada and her people to cherish
and manifest at the present juncture of our affairs.

www.ingramcontent.com/pod-product-compliance
Lightning Source LLC
Chambersburg PA
CBHW031823090426
42739CB00008B/1381